" In a rapidly changing world it is rare that someone can touch ones life in such a powerfully positive way. Thomas McMillan is that someone, he writes with knowledge, compassion and reasoning that are rarely found. His grasp of mental health, reasoning, love and life will leave the reader feeling settled, focused with a deeper understanding of themselves. If there is one book you read this year read Thomas's.......it will change your life"

Martin Nulty
Business Leader and Entrepreneur

" This fine collection of overflowing positivity from Thomas is long overdue. I remember him and I discussing areas of mutual concern in relation to how central we felt it was for young people to develop the positive mindsets that will manage trials and tribulations charecteristic of much contemporary living, and so, enhance our ability to make choices that deliver positive outcomes.

Thomas' writing has been inspired by his late father, also named Thomas (RIP), who believed in the importance of positive thinking to overcome obstacles and many of Thomas' motivational quotations have their genesis in narratives originally developed by his Dad. It is clear to me that Thomas' father had a hugely positive influence on him and this is demonstrated in the quality of the beautifully inspiring work of art he has lovingly created in the pages of this work. "

Frank Devine
Social Worker and Team Leader

" Having known Thomas for many years I've always been aware of his ability to motivate and inspire with his quirky quotes and well thought writings, I knew it was only a matter of time before he brought about a book such as these in one collective place.
Thomas is a natural motivator and I personally look forward to reading his daily quotes before I set about my day.......
I sincerely hope you do too ! "

John Terry
Former Chelsea & England Captain & Aston Villa Assistant Manager

"If you can apply your focus to what you can do, you need not worry about what you can't."

T K McMillan

Too often we consume ourselves with our "can't do's" in life instead of focusing on where our greatest strengths lie. Dreams will grow when we add activity to thought, look at what you CAN DO today to make a start in chasing your Goal(s).

My Day /

"Sometimes change happens not because that's what you want, but because that's what you need."

T K McMillan

Situations occur in our lives which we may question, paths we are on suddenly change……….but in time it is revealed that in fact this diversion is exactly what we may have needed.

My Day /

"Always stay strong and hold a belief that you can make it."

T K McMillan

When we have experienced a setback it is natural to take a knock personally and to feel some form of deflation in our journey, however it is essential this stumble is analyzed specifically to see what growth is to be gained from it, whilst retaining clear focus in our quest for ultimate success."

My Day /

"You will not achieve a positive outcome with a negative approach."

T K McMillan

We may not be in control of everything that can happen to us in a day........but we are in control of how we react to it.
Stay in control of YOU throughout your day and try, where possible, to apply your most positive thinking to any situation.

My Day /

"You don't have to be the tallest in your field to be the most respected, but you DO have to walk tall!"

T K McMillan

It's very easy to hold our head up high when things are going your way but walking tall when things are going against you, when you haven't felt success in a while........that's when the measure of your self belief will be tested.

My Day/

"As sure as you will change your clothing daily, you must also remain flexible enough to change your thinking and your habits."

T K McMillan

Be prepared to work, not just harder on yourself, but smarter.........be ready to adapt and to be better than you were yesterday.

My Day /

"Your dream can come to life, if you will only take time to breathe air into it."

T K McMillan

Have you given your dreams and goals the opportunity of fulfilment, have you really pursued them, or are they simply passive thoughts?

My Day /

"Nothing is lost until it is given up."

T K McMillan

You are not defeated until you have decided to try no more, until you have lost the purpose you set out within your heart.

My Day /

"Failure is part of the process, not part of you."

T K McMillan

Understanding failure, and the fear of it, will really help you grow........understanding that if you are to see success then failure must also play its part.
Do not give up at the hint of a fall, dust yourself down and move on speedily..........

My Day /

"Action, not words, changes lives."

T K McMillan

We can talk all day, enthuse our opinion, force our views even..........but unless we get to work nothing will change. We must become active in our pursuits, sitting around will not get the job done.

My Day /

"If you're going to hit the back of the net, you're going to have to shoot sometime."

T K McMillan

We can put off taking up the reins or facing our greatest fears for a time but unless we commit to taking a risk we will spend many a day filled with regret.

My Day /

"Stand with the guys who are prepared to stand with you."

T K McMillan

Surround yourself with people who's opinions you value and respect, who will give you the necessary advice and critique that will assist you in your journey, and who care about you enough to offer a shoulder when you need it.

My Day /

"The joy lies in the journey."

T K McMillan

We all embrace the success and the trophy's but, on reflection, the greatest joy lies in the rounds we had to endure to get to presentation day.
Embrace your journey, for there lies much greater fulfilment than the medals you pick up along the way.

My Day /

"Who you wish to become is ultimately down to you, it is the responsibility of no one else."

T K McMillan

You cannot leave your dreams in the hands of another........you must be the driver, you must steer the ship and you must fuel the fire to ensure you become the person your talent deserves.

My Day /

"If you haven't found a solution yet, keep asking questions."

T K McMillan

As in business and in life, the answers won't always come at the first time of asking, so we must be prepared to look further into the abyss and go in search again.

My Day /

"With the correct application, we can ALL be awesome in our own unique way."

T K McMillan

When you set out to develop yourself in a specific area or field, it makes great sense to be first aware of the level you wish to achieve and the skills you may require........as well as who's help and guidance you may require along the way.

My Day /

"See yourself in a new world of existence."

T K McMillan

Have you yet tested your mind to see how far your imagination will extend and the true depth of your ambitions and goals? Look at your future, at the desires that burn within you........and just how hard you're prepared to work to bring these passions to life.

My Day /

"Every success story is owned by someone who once had a dream."

T K McMillan

Some people are happy to wander through life in rounds of repetition, repeating daily chores without a conscious vision of the possibilities that we may find possible to reach......are YOU one of them or are you going to take a moment now to consider YOUR dream........?

My Day /

"Dig a little deeper, that's where the oil lies."

T K McMillan

Just when you think you're on your last breath, when your efforts are running low.......dig that little bit deeper and bring out that last minute of fight that separates the Champions from the contenders.

My Day /

"Building something of significance will only happen when the foundations are secure."

T K McMillan

Nothing lasts the test of time unless it comes from well prepared foundations. If you can do your best to ensure the greatest preparation......your success story stands a chance of lasting longer than the first two chapters.

My Day /

"People fail not because they don't KNOW what's needed, but because they don't DO what's needed."

T K McMillan

We often are able to see where a problem lies, sometimes even holding aloft the solution, but unless we get busy doing something about it, the wheels will keep turning and the problem shall remain.

My Day /

"Money you can win back, time you cannot."

T K McMillan

We use time more freely than we use money, often not respecting it or investing it doing the things we should be doing.......in the end will your memories reflect time well spent or money?"

My Day /

"YOU are your point of difference."

T K McMillan

In a world engulfed with copies, re-makes, second editions and fakes it's important to remember the uniqueness of YOU.......you are a one off, there will be no re-casting of you when you're gone, no new model to fill your shoes.
This is your time, make it all that it can be.

My Day /

"Do what needs to be done to get you to where you need to go."

T K McMillan

In simple terms, you have to be committed and determined to outwork any of your direct competitors, to work harder and smarter than you did the day before and to engulf yourself in the dream that you hold so dear in your hands.

My Day /

"Are you working towards something.........or are you just working?"

T K McMillan

Can you honestly say at this moment you have a definitive plan of action with any resemblance of a map laid out for which you may progress on a day to day basis.........or are you just wandering in hope?"

My Day /

"Progress is everything."

T K McMillan

Regardless of pace, what is most important is that progress is being made, that we are not standing still or accepting a decline.........because remember, that is what saw off the dinosaur.

My Day /

"Some days seem easy, some seem tough but placing them all in the pot allows us just the right mix."

T K McMillan

There are days where you are simply flying and others where you feel like you just can't get off the ground ....but without the days of digging deep and learning, you will not gain the experience required to give you that pilot's licence.

My Day /

"In many we are blessed with sight, but it doesn't always mean we have the ability to see."

T K McMillan

For so many of us we are fortunate not to be blind but does that mean we are looking out for the vision that will propel us........or are we just staring into the darkness?!

My Day /

"Activate your dream."

T K McMillan

Much of the time we wait without reason, possibly through fear of failure........but in fact there is no conceivable, tangible reason to delay any longer.........get yourself going now!

My Day /

"If you won't take a risk you'll never win the prize."

T K McMillan

You cannot expect to win the competition if you won't at least take part. Don't immerse yourself in the reasons you won't win, just think about what could happen if you did!

My Day /

"It's one thing climbing the mountain, it's a completely different matter staying there long enough to enjoy the view."

T K McMillan

As our pathway is developing and we are chasing down the dream, our enthusiasm and sense of purpose is at its peak...........but can you sustain it once you've reached that Goal?

My Day /

"The desire must be greater than the fear."

T K McMillan

Our reason, our purpose, the people we are doing it for (ourselves included)........all these reasons must be greater than the fear that is holding us back.

My Day /

"The reason the ocean's carry such power is because they do not know how to stop moving forward."

T K McMillan

If you have the ability to keep moving forward, even in the toughest of times, you will make it to your destination when all else have long since given up.

My Day /

"If you're going to spend your time consumed by something, make sure it's something you love."

T K McMillan

We are each blessed to be gifted 24 hours each day.......are we spending them with a deliberate enthusiasm and gratitude or are we just taking for granted another passing day?

My Day /

"Let today be the first day."

T K McMillan

Every major change in our lives must begin with a starting point, a point at which we introduce adjustments and new habits into our lives.........and that starting point must begin with YOU."

My Day /

"If you can touch the heart, you can reach the soul."

T K McMillan

If you can take enough interest in another person to reach their heart, you will be allowed the luxury of getting to know them from the depths of their soul.......but be warned, this trust must too be valued.

My Day /

"We don't have to reach the bottom to decide we want to climb to the top."

T K McMillan

Deciding to stop doing what you are doing, to take away the pain you are currently suffering, doesn't necessitate that you reach the depths of hell first........you can decide to change now!

My Day /

"How far we can reach will depend on how far we can see.

T K McMillan

Too often we pitch our ambitions way too low, lacking the belief to envisage the type of life that is in fact available to us all...........it's out there, it can be reached you know.

My Day /

"Plan for the future, but live in the now."

T K McMillan

How often do you actually take time out to live in the specific moment you stand.......take a slow breath now, take in your surroundings, and most of all, enjoy the people who stand with you?!

My Day /

"Remember, a Phoenix is born from the ashes."

T K McMillan

Always keep clear in your mind, even when all hope seems lost and you feel there is nowhere else to turn.........that there is always another chance out there, waiting for YOU to give it a go!

My Day /

"To thy own self be true."

Thomas McMillan Snr

Regardless of where we are at or what is going on in our lives, we must always remain true to ourselves, to our conscience and to behave in a manner that fits with our inner beliefs.

My Day /

"Don't build walls, build bridges."

T K McMillan

When things are going against us, when our trust has been breached, we often become defensive and close the walls around us......build bridges, hold friends and family dear, grow beyond the place you find yourself now.

My Day /

"There are no good times or bad times, there is only time.....and how we choose to use it."

T K McMillan

Too often we feel sorry for ourselves when things are building against us, we're let down or under pressure.......other times we have the world at our feet and are in total control, but it is all a state of mind that WE can control with applied focus.

My Day /

"Sometimes you need a rock in the road to direct you onto the right path."

T K McMillan

It sometimes causes us alarm when we are moved off our current route, especially when we think things are going well........but to get us to a better destination this is often just what we need.

My Day /

"If you want to help someone on their way, guide them to the entrance of the tunnel, not the light at the end of it."

T K McMillan

Helping people can be a delicate operation but remember, it shouldn't turn into an ego trip about who you are, it's simply about them finding out who they are.

My Day /

"Implementing change only requires that you take the first step."

T K McMillan

It is not enough to change our thinking alone, we must also be prepared to change our actions.

My Day /

"The road of self discovery begins the moment you leave your comfort zone."

T K McMillan

We cannot hang on to the past, we cannot hide from opportunity based on our momentary fears.......we must break from the leash and give life the fullest of go's."

My Day /

"Don't avoid your fears........address them."

T K McMillan

There are times in all our lives when we feel the desire to bury our heads in the sand and avoid facing tough tests. But we can't, we have to dust ourselves down, get the head lifted, shoulders back, and go face up to our responsibilities.

My Day /

"To reach the top table you must be prepared to climb all the stairs."

T K McMillan

There is no easy way, no elevator to success, you must put in the hours, dedicate yourself and retain the self discipline to see the job through to its end.

My Day /

"The moment we decide where we are in life is no longer where we care to be............our lives will change."

T K McMillan

Committing to yourself that you are no longer happy accepting the mundane will ensure that you will do something about improving your life as it is in this moment.

My Day /

"Nobody cares too much about where you started, it's where you'll finish that attracts their interest."

T K McMillan

Regardless of our backgrounds or starting points, we all have the opportunity to grow and flourish, we all have the right to become a success.

My Day /

"It's easy to see the path on the sunny days, but how clear is it in the torrential rain?"

T K McMillan

When we are winning, when success is at hand, it is very easy to see our route ahead but what of the dark days, the tougher one's........the days where life is not seeming so easy?!"

My Day /

"If you're prepared to go further than you've ever been, you'll get to see things you've never seen."

T K McMillan

If we will stretch ourselves that little bit further, take on the challenges we've avoided in the past, we just never know how fulfilling our lives can become and of how high we can fly."

My Day /

"If we can control our thinking, we will control our actions."

T K McMillan

If we are able to retain positivity, if we are able to retain clarity in our thinking and in our planning, our actions will remain focused and on track........even in the toughest of times.

My Day /

"Success lies in the DO-ING."

T K McMillan

Make a plan, have an end in mind, and work it till you see the sunshine break through the horizon. Success is held in your hands, if you will just give it a chance.

My Day /

"Wouldn't you dare to just do things that little bit differently?"

T K McMillan

The heroes in our lives, the idols we hold dear........were they conformists, did they stick to the straight lines, what makes them stand out from the crowd?
Nothing dictates we have to follow like sheep, we too can make a new path.

My Day /

"A feeling of despair will only remain so long as we choose to do nothing about it."

T K McMillan

Too often we repeatedly play a horror moment in our minds over and over.......when we should address it at the earliest possible moment, allowing us to move on and clear our thoughts for something with greater purpose.

My Day /

"We are but what we choose to be."

T K McMillan

Who we are, and who we may become, is decided by us alone........our commitment and dedication to becoming a person of value depends on the depths of our ambitions.

My Day /

"The only person you have to prove it to is YOU."

T K McMillan

I read many motivational posts about proving others in your life wrong........don't apply your focus on their thoughts, apply it to yours."

My Day /

"It's not the years in our life that matter so much, but the life in our years."

T K McMillan

We can repeat the same day....day in, day out, and end with a blandness of existence........but that's not what we're here for, that's not what lies available to us.

My Day /

"Reaching the end of one particular road doesn't mean the journey is over, it means simply that you have surpassed that milestone and it is time to set a brand new goal."

T K McMillan

We can work hard to achieve a particular success or trophy but it doesn't signify the end.....it only confirms that when we set a goal, we achieve it.......and that it is now time to move on.

My Day /

"If you can't see yourself at the top of the mountain, why would you bother to take the first step?"

T K McMillan

If you are not driven, if you hold no ambitions, then what are your expectations, what is it that drives you out of bed in the morning and where lies your purpose?

My Day /

"It is in times of great adversity that our deepest resolve is discovered."

T K McMillan

Sometimes when our back is against the wall, and when we face our greatest tests, we only then come out fighting, pushing with passion to an ultimately successful conclusion.

My Day /

"You weren't born to stand in, you were born to stand out."

T K McMillan

Regardless of where our greatest passions lie we can be the best there is at that particular profession or hobby, because in the end, who sets out to be second best anyway?

My Day /

"Your mind is your greatest asset, feed it well and it will blossom like the greatest flower."

T K McMillan

Just as the saying goes........what goes in develops what will come back out. Be cautious with your thinking and control what you feed the mind so the output you desire is exactly what you get.

My Day /

"To share is to know, and to give is to grow."

T K McMillan

The greatest blessing is to be able to share........your knowledge, your worth, your wealth and your soul.......and the luxury of being in a position to pass on something of value to a neighbour who needs it.

My Day /

"He who sees the joy in living will find the passage to eternal life."

T K McMillan

Explore, enjoy and be thankful, many people would swap places with you in a heartbeat.

My Day /

"Take where you've gone wrong in the past and use it to ensure you will get it right in the future."

T K McMillan

It is human nature to make mistakes, to have errors of judgement or trust, but if we make no changes to our thoughts or behaviors the lessons will go unlearned.

My Day /

"Do what drives you, not what drags you along."

T K McMillan

We only have one go on the merry go round, we are not here for false starts or for wasted opportunity, we are here to give it our absolute level best and for the things that lift our heart.

My Day /

"Be believable."

T K McMillan

To gain the trust of others we must offer sincerity and show something worth believing in, and from there people will buy into the dream we project.

My Day /

"Allow yourself time to be a success, nobody actually did it overnight"

T K McMillan

Many of our idols may appear to have become an overnight success but in most cases they had many days of disappointment.......before they could become that overnight success.

My Day /

"Embrace education, it's a gift we receive so that in time we can offer."

T K McMillan

We must always remain open to learning, and likewise we must also be available to pass on our message to the future generations who will come behind us."

My Day /

"What we can achieve will only be determined by how much it means to us and how hard we're prepared to work to get there."

T K McMillan

If something is so powerful in our minds and in our hearts we will make the time, put in the extra work, and never give up until that dream has been realized."

My Day /

"Dreams are an introduction to the life we want to lead."

T K McMillan

Our dreams and ambitions do not need to be a far away thought distanced from the grasps of extended hands.........we can be anything we dream of if we will just dare to go after it.

My Day /

"Just when it appears that it can't be done........DO IT! The world is there to be proven wrong."

T K McMillan

We've all faced tests we thought we couldn't overcome only to face that moment when we broke through, finding the challenge wasn't so impossible after all."

My Day /

"In the pits of darkness be the light that shines through."

T K McMillan

Be it in your own life or in that of a neighbour, YOU can be the one that shines light upon the dullest of moments.

My Day /

"Do not allow errors in the past to define who you shall become in the future."

T K McMillan

We afford too much time in our heads re-running failures of our past, instead of focusing on changing what we need to guarantee a better future.

My Day /

"Today's beginning doesn't have to be tomorrow's end."

T K McMillan

It is more important we get started on a journey than standing with anticipation. The talk won't get us there, only the walk will do so….. And for that we must make a start!

My Day /

"You have the time and you have the talent, the rest depends on how you use them."

T K McMillan

We often put off the work required in exchange for something of ease, playtime even........but this will not take you closer to your destination or Goal or see your talents used in their most purposeful fashion.

My Day /

"The journey has no purpose without an end in mind."

T K McMillan

It's very easy to lose a lot of time when traveling without direction, without purpose or no end product but when you have a destination at the forefront of your mind everything serves with a much greater power.

My Day /

"Where we are headed is of far greater importance than the route that will take us there."

T K McMillan

Even if we are taken off track now and again, we will not lose sight of the target we are going to achieve and the enthusiasm that carries us towards our ultimate Goal.

My Day /

"Live a little."

T K McMillan

It's very easy to get caught up in the daily runnings of life, to such an extent that we forget to LIVE, and instead begin to simply exist.

My Day /

"Will you control the day or will the day control you?"

T K McMillan

As you set out each morning to go at another day, what plans have you in mind, what will you achieve from the next 24 hours.........is it maybe time to give that some thought?

My Day /

"You're greatest strengths will reveal themselves when you are in your darkest days."

T K McMillan

In our deepest moments of despair we will either find the strength to fight back or we will not.....
And the answer to that question is one that only WE can answer.

My Day /

"One of the greatest aspects of the game of life is that, even after a defeat, you get to play again."

T K McMillan

Sometimes the days are tough, some of the them can really set us back........but the game isn't over there, tomorrow you get to roll the dice all over again.

My Day /

"Today is a new day, a chance to start the journey afresh."

T K McMillan

Failure is temporary, don't carry it as a backpack, learn to let it go and start again.

My Day /

"What you say and how you act will come from from your perspective, how people choose to receive it will come from theirs."

T K McMillan

We can only act in a manner cohesive to our beliefs, if people don't grasp the sincerity of it then that will be a problem we can do little about.

My Day /

"Grasp the moment, seize your chance."

T K McMillan

When that opportunity comes knocking you need to be prepared to jump and be ready to say YES!

My Day /

"Discovering the treasure is the reward for the time, dedication and effort in searching for it."

T K McMillan

Each day we go out searching for our ultimate moments, our greatest ambitions both personally and professionally.......if we keep on trying they will reveal themselves in the goodness of time.

My Day /

"If your focus remains on the destination you won't become bogged down by the length of the journey."

T K McMillan

If you have a Goal you are committed to there is absolutely nothing that will stop you from reaching it, as long as the vision is strong enough.

My Day /

"Build from where you stand today, not from where you once stood in the past."

T K McMillan

Don't get caught up in your past moments of glory, you are where you stand right now and that is the only place you can progress from.

My Day /

"What we repeatedly feed our brain will become the nature of our behavior, so guard your thoughts with care."

T K McMillan

Negative thinking creeps up on us when we least expect it........one little niggle of doubt quickly developing into fear. Focus on what you WANT, not what on you want to avoid.

My Day /

"One loss doesn't end the season, as long as you bounce back from it the title can still be yours."

T K McMillan

Fall down, skin your knees.......but you get back up and don't waste any time about it.

My Day /

"Own your days."

T K McMillan

You can decide to retain control of your day or you can allow someone else's actions to do so, but that will only occur with your permission.

My Day /

"The strength of our mind will determine the outcome of our actions."

T K McMillan

Meaningful, purposeful thinking will produce constructive, decisive actions. Practice that until it becomes habitual.

My Day /

"What have you got to lose?"

T K McMillan

Fear prevents action, which in turn causes anxiety. If this is the outcome of doing nothing what are the possibilities out there if we'll just try to do something?

My Day /

"Don't become busy just being busy........this isn't how progress is made."

T K McMillan

Our days can become so consumed doing our general day to day activities that we end up in a repetition of time, which delays progress. We must find 'time out' to review our plan and review our activity as often as we can.

My Day /

"There are days when our determination to succeed can do no more than exceed our fear of failure."

T K McMillan

We don't have all the answers, and there are some days that feels more overpowering than others, however if our determination hangs strong we will get there just the same.

My Day /

"If I can only let go of yesterday I may be open to the discovery of tomorrow."

T K McMillan

Treat life on that basis, take each day as it comes and allow it to start afresh, do not bog it down with matters you can no longer do anything about.

My Day /

"Don't become the obstacle in the way of winning your own race."

T K McMillan

Many roadblocks will meet you throughout your journey but be assured YOU are not one of them. Don't allow your thinking to hold you back, push on in the knowledge that you can be a winner too.

My Day /

"Some doors will benefit us if they simply don't open, the one's we really need are just a bit further down the line."

T K McMillan

We can all be disappointed with what appears to be a failure or a hope unrealized, but it may just be that there is something better waiting round the corner."

My Day /

"Contentment is knowing you are in the right place, it is not a lack of ambition."

T K McMillan

When you feel at peace with where you are it doesn't mean you don't have a desire to elevate yourself to somewhere higher, it just confirms that you know you are happy within.

My Day /

"Sometimes we need to take a long, hard look around us and just be grateful for what, and who, we have in life........there is always someone who'd gladly fill our shoes."

T K McMillan

Gratitude is never a bad place to start, especially when we are feeling a wee bit sorry for ourselves.

My Day /

"Regardless of your age or stage, there is so much out there awaiting your endeavor."

T K McMillan

Sometimes we feel too young, at times we believe we are too old.......but if you have the ambition and the work ethic age is definitely but a number.

My Day /

"Too often we gauge our progress against those we see locally, publicly and particularly on social media........but our only real competition is looking back at us every morning when we brush our teeth."

T K McMillan

Don't get caught up with false Gods, people we see but do not touch, it's only our own journey that we have to work on developing.

My Day /

"I am still living and breathing, therefore my dream is still alive."

T K McMillan

It ain't over till you stop trying....that hope, that passion and that energy is still in there and bursting to get out if you'll just give it a chance.

My Day /

"Prepare for failure but get ready for success."

T K McMillan

We'll have those let downs along the way but they only serve as part of our learning whilst our destination of success awaits our arrival.

My Day /

"Great experiences are available to us all, they are not reserved for the chosen few."

T K McMillan

Remember that you hold equal value, you are no better or worse than the person you stand shoulder to shoulder with..........the highest level of happiness is available for you too.

My Day /

"When you set out on your journey in the morning you know where you are headed to, but you are available to change the route if you run in to traffic."

T K McMillan

By now we may have an idea where we are aiming to go but we may have to occasionally adjust the course from time to time.......be available to that.

My Day /

"Wisdom is only wasted on the old If the gifts aren't passed down the line."

T K McMillan

We must share up and down the line......spend time with people of various ages and you will be sure to share some special moments.

My Day /

"Make sure you get some colour about you before the sun sets."

T K McMillan

Value your time, value your friends and family and most of all.........live every single day as though it's going to be your last.

My Day /

"What if you were guaranteed to make it, if you knew it was a sure thing........how hard would you work then?"

T K McMillan

Sometimes we hold back a little for the fear of falling flat in public.....but would you really throw yourself at your dream if you knew you could reach it......

My Day /

"Sweet dreams."

T K McMillan

Before you let the sun set give yourself one positive thought to carry into the next day, give your dreams a chance to become your reality and start tonight's dreaming off with a clear vision of the life you pray for.

My Day /

"Why not me?"

T K McMillan

What is it in your mind that convinces you that YOU are not worthy of reaching the highest of stars, what is it that makes you believe you cannot become more than your current climate suggests?

My Day /

"If your mindset is that of a winner, a winner you shall be."

T K McMillan

If your focus is firmly on succeeding and winning the race the negativity will not find a route through to penetrating the mind.

My Day /

"We all wake up with doubts, but we must fight against them or they will paralyze us with fear."

T K McMillan

It is normal human behavior to experience doubt and fear but it is only in the mind.......we can replace that feeling with belief and take action to get our Goal going again.

My Day /

"Don't confuse the trivial with the important."

T K McMillan

Don't allow your time to be eaten up dealing with things that are of little importance. Prioritize your weekly timetable and apply yourself where it serves best.

My Day /

"We all need a mentor in life, a guiding light........someone to look up to."

T K McMillan

Find someone in your life you admire, someone that you respect and someone who's path is similar to the one which you would like to follow.

My Day /

"Seek out a role model who will work with you, someone you trust and someone who's opinion you value."

T K McMillan

When selecting a role model be patient, be choosy, pick someone who you hold in the highest esteem.

My Day /

"To read is to explore the mind, to take yourself on a journey of your own imagination."

T K McMillan

We must read as often as possible, one book of a hobby and one of education.......it keeps the mind alert and allows you to tap into fields unknown.

My Day /

"Expanding our own minds and improving our own education is the greatest gift we can ever give to ourselves."

T K McMillan

Make a point of learning something new every day, stretch yourself and stretch your mind.

My Day /

"It is not enough to know your stuff.........if you want to be heard you must learn to express yourself in a manner that people will want to listen to."

T K McMillan

People will only hear you if they find interest in what you have to say.......work on your delivery and work on yourself.

My Day /

"He who listens always learns more."

T K McMillan

We are all guilty of the desire to first express our own views, but how often do we actually genuinely listen to the words of another........or are we simply waiting for another opportunity to speak?

My Day /

"If it matters enough, you'll find a way."

T K McMillan

When you are passionate about something, and you just know that it's got to be done, you'll find a way."

My Day /

"Who we can become depends upon the vision we hold in our hearts and in our minds,"

T K McMillan

If you can dream, if you can set Goals, there is no end to how much you can achieve.........all you need now is a little bit of action.

My Day /

"It's ok to be a little bit weird, people who stand out normally are."

T K McMillan

We don't always have to look to fit in with the crowd, it's ok to be a little bit different, to be unique. Trust in who you are and don't be swayed into the sheep.

My Day /

"We don't have to be products of our background, that's not where our future lies."

T K McMillan

People can attempt to label us because of where we have come from but that will only carry if we allow it to be the case. Our lives don't exist in the past, they exist in our future.

My Day /

"With the resources available to us all these days there really is no excuse for not being able to access the help we need."

T K McMillan

I absolutely accept we don't all have computers, laptops or tablets etc but there are people and places who are only too happy to help.

My Day /

"Would you be happier using your energy explaining why you CAN'T do something or use it proving YOU can?"

T K McMillan

Too often we take up as much time and energy making excuses to avoid a bit of extra effort than we do just getting on with the job at hand.

My Day /

"If we won't put in what's required to make our live's unique they won't be........they will only be what we choose to make them."

T K McMillan

Don't wait for someone else to make it happen for you, pick up the reins and steer yourself into the exact path of your choosing.

My Day /

"If we won't put in what's required to make our live's unique they won't be........they will only be what we choose to make them."

T K McMillan

Don't wait for someone else to make it happen for you, pick up the reins and steer yourself into the exact path of your choosing.

My Day /

"I have many a regret, but none of them are down to inactivity."

T K McMillan

Of course we will not go through life without regret, but make sure your regret's are not for having tried your absolute best.

My Day /

"Before you treat someone's time with disregard, consider first what it has cost them."

T K McMillan

It's very easy to be wasteful with another's time or goods but please be aware of both the cost to us AND the cost to them.

My Day/

"I care little for those who care nothing for me."

T K McMillan

We should not spend time chasing people who offer nothing to our lives, the people in our circle who's focus lies solely upon their own well being...........these are not the people who will encourage the progression of YOU!

My Day /

"If history proves one thing, it is that everybody has a chance to win."

T K McMillan

Look at our heroes of the past, look at the one's who defied the odds.......if they proved it possible, so may we.

My Day /

"Who said YOU weren't good enough?"

T K McMillan

Don't be held back by the fears of another, your opinion is the only one YOU should be listening to, not that of anyone else.

My Day /

"Being born out of a great house is no where near as important as being part of a great home."

T K McMillan

The house we leave every day may be grand in stature but the home we can contribute to is of such greater meaning.

My Day /

"Gratitude leaves the room the moment expectation enters it."

T K McMillan

That point where people's gratitude for what you have done for them slips away as they begin to expect from you……. don't be used beyond a point that you are comfortable with.

My Day /

"What difference do YOU make to the problem?"

T K McMillan

Do you make a problem grow like a tumor or do you help to remove it from all existence?"

It is of course far easier to go along with gossip and hearsay of poor value but if you are aware of a solution, why not throw it into the ring?

My Day /

"Talk all you like, but people buy into the progress they can see."

T K McMillan

Achievement is a thing people should voice about what you show, it is not something you should voice about what you think.

My Day /

"Avoid people of a loud and aggressive nature, they know no other way to express themselves."

Thomas McMillan Snr

When people can't express what they feel they often react with aggression of some sort........it's worth noting that very little is ever achieved, or truly respected, this way.

My Day /

"If you can bring one thing to the group..........bring YOU."

T K McMillan

Don't turn up displaying anyone but you, that's the only person you really have."

My Day /

"I am capable not only of change, but of creating change."

T K McMillan

The example we set when we are prepared to show visible changes to how we exist is primarily of benefit to us, but what of the example it sets..........?!

My Day /

"To be a winner you must first be prepared to do what your competitors are not prepared to do."

T K McMillan

If we are so driven that our actions see our competition stop half way, it is sure that we will be first on the mantle.

My Day /

"If you are good enough that first place may be a consideration, why would you possibly see second place as being ok?"

T K McMillan

If you can succeed, if you can reach the Goal of your choosing, why would you then be prepared to accept something considerably less?

My Day /

"If now is your time, take up the reins and drive forward with conviction."

T K McMillan

There is no other reason for delay beyond excuse, why would you treat yourself in such a fashion, why would you not allow yourself to succeed in the manner you thoroughly deserve?

My Day /

"If we can only raise our expectations."

T K McMillan

If we cannot at least display a desire and a passion for our personal, self improvement, what chance do we really have?

My Day/

"Who we can become depends not on how we view ourselves at the beginning, but in who we are to become at the end."

T K McMillan

How we personally see ourselves, how great we may see our achievements, will depend largely on the successes we believe lies within us.

My Day/

"We are who we are, and that can be everything we'll ever need."

T K McMillan

Sometimes you have to look within yourself, finding the strength of depth to know that YOU are good enough, that what you bring to the table has value.

My Day /

"If you can't find the time to invest in yourself how can you expect anyone else to?"

T K McMillan

If you won't set aside the time to invest in improving your own mind, your own education and your own self development.........how can you very well expect anyone else to?

My Day /

"Once you make a commitment, a dedication to fulfilling a plan, your life starts to change beyond your imagination."

T K McMillan

We can talk till we are blue in the face but the moment that brings about real change is the moment you commit.

My Day /

"Have you yet explored the possibilities available to you, have you looked specifically at what you could achieve with your unique talent?"

T K McMillan

Just for a moment, consider what would happen to you if you started to invest in your dream.

My Day /

"Of course you can be strong, what's the alternative?"

T K McMillan

When we feel the greatest pressures, when we feel the walls are closing in, we must apply our thinking to the solution, NOT to the problem, and from there we'll work our way out of the darkness.

My Day /

"When I take part I take part with all that I have, otherwise why would I take part at all."

T K McMillan

If you are going to apply yourself, don't do it half heartedly, don't do it without care or passion.....
Do your very best as frequently as you possibly can.

My Day /

"I am going to make it, for that is the decision I have come to."

T K McMillan

Apply yourself to your dream, work it, enthuse it, bring it to life.

My Day /

"Take time out to look not only at what you are doing day to day, but to look at what you could be doing day to day."

T K McMillan

I know your life may be busy, I know it may be difficult to find the time to invest in your dream......
But, put simply, you must find that time someway, somehow.

My Day /

"You'll be amazed at what you can achieve with no more than sheer determination."

T K McMillan

When you will not give up, when you decide to overcome every obstacle, there is simply no end to what you can achieve.

My Day /

"Our fight must come from within."

T K McMillan

We must find the depth of strength to face up to the tests, we must also ensure we are feeding our mind the right information, so that it may prepare us best for the challenges ahead.

My Day /

"If you will extend me your hand I will greatly receive it."

T K McMillan

Too often we feel too embarrassed to seek the help or assistance of another, this will only serve to make our journey all the slower.........drop the ego and look out for help, there's no shame in support.

My Day /

"I too can become a leader."

T K McMillan

With the right preparation, desire and enthusiasm you can be the one to direct the flock, you too can become the guide in the field.

My Day /

"My desire today is to be one step ahead of where I was yesterday."

T K McMillan

Progress, large and small, is progress none the less. Make sure today is a day where you took another step...........

My Day /

"If you can see life through an open mind the view will be one of far greater value."

T K McMillan

It's the safest place on earth to sit behind YOUR opinion but where will that take you, what will you learn or gain from life that you don't already know...............and will your life experience be as fulfilling as you can be afforded.

My Day /

"If we can learn to listen with as much passion as we talk we will reach new levels of learning."

T K McMillan

Frequently we are not actually listening but merely waiting on our opportunity to pitch in our view.........learn to listen to people in a committed way and you will be amazed at what you very rarely hear.

My Day /

"People need to see something in you with which they can connect........give them that reason."

T K McMillan

When people look at you they want to see something they can buy in to, something believable and integrity that makes for more than a short term relationship.

My Day /

"If our actions can come close to backing up our speech our journey shall be one of value."

T K McMillan

It is not enough to simply talk a good game, we must be sure we are prepared for the work proving our road ahead is the one we speak of.

My Day /

"If we won't give it our all we'll never know quite what we could become."

T K McMillan

Why go at something with a half-hearted effort, why bother trying at all if you're not going to give it all that you can.............don't embarrass yourself or let yourself down by showing less than you are capable of.

My Day /

"The future you shall be constructed from the foundations of today."

T K McMillan

If you hold dreams and aspirations for the future there is no greater time to lay the first blocks in the ground than now, no reason to wait, no reason to waste a second longer. Your future will be a representation of the work you put in now.

My Day /

"Who's to say where you could be a year from now.........YOU, that's who!

T K McMillan

If you will not be the Captain of your own ship......the guide of your own destiny, then who will?

My Day /

"Turn your Dreams into your reality be setting measurable Goals."

T K McMillan

Lay your ambitions out in front of you, draw up a plan with regular milestones to help keep you on track and bring your dreams to life.

My Day /

"Some storms last longer than others, but none lasts forever."

T K McMillan

Turbulent days will try us, they may even push us to our limits but if we hold on to the vision we are in pursuit of, the sunny days will shine again.

My Day /

"There can be no one more deserved of basking in your success than those who have supported you through your failures."

T K McMillan

When that Goal is reached, when you access the dizzy heights of success, remember who helped get you there and share the joy with them.

My Day /

"If there is little passion, there is little point."

T K McMillan

To exercise a dream, to bring it to life......you must have enthusiasm and passion for it, you must be the one who is going to drive it, and you must show it with all that you possess.

My Day /

"As the gas starts to run low, make sure you are happy with the miles that you have travelled."

T K McMillan

There is no room in life for regret, we either win or we learn..........and as long as we learn we'll win in the end.

My Day /

"All the answers aren't always available but if we continue to search, and ask the right questions, they will soon reveal themselves."

T K McMillan

We don't know everything, we don't always have all the information at hand but what we need we can find, we can look for, and we can ask for the assistance of others.

My Day /

"Imagine what you could become."

T K McMillan

With a little bit more effort, and a little bit of smarter planning, just imagine what you could turn into............scary isn't it?

My Day /

"In life.......there's always a way to move forward."

T K McMillan

Sometimes our problems may seem insurmountable but out there someone is facing challenges way above those of our own, tests we should feel lucky to live without.........so roll up your sleeves, shake off the dust, and get ready to go to work.

My Day /

"If we stop once we've progressed from a crawl to a walk, we will never learn to run."

T K McMillan

A little success is just that......a little. Don't settle for one small victory but instead, use it as a launch pad to propel you to the very next level.

My Day /

"If you can apply focus to where you have talent, you need worry less about where you do not."

T K McMillan

Too often we focus on what we are not capable of doing but what matters more is where we do have talent, where our passions lie and what we may achieve with these gifts. Focus on your strengths and develop them as best you can.

My Day /

"Success involves failure."

T K McMillan

We will get it wrong, we will fail sometimes but the game isn't up until the last whistle is blown so understand failure, and the need for it.........and then use it to fuel your success.

My Day /

"What matters most is our happiness in who we are from within, what matters less is the need to prove it to others."

T K McMillan

We can consume our time trying to prove to others that we are happy, that we fit in and are equal to those around us...........but actually the thing that matters most is that we are truly happy within ourselves.

My Day /

"Seek out a role model who will help you, someone you trust, and someone who's opinion you value."

T K McMillan

Work with people of value, people who's journey you wish to emulate.

My Day /

"Plan for the future, live in the now."

T K McMillan

We must give thought to our plan, our Goals and our ways of getting down that path towards them but we must always remember to live for the moment........we just never know how precious they are when we're in them.

My Day /

"To thy own self be true."

T McMillan Snr

Remain true to yourself, to your beliefs, to your integrity........do not short change who you are for anyone.

My Day /

"If we can get a plane off the ground then so too we can our dreams."

T K McMillan

It is incredible to understand what it takes to take the weight of steel in an airplane and lift it from the ground successfully........if we can make that happen then so too we can our dreams.

My Day /

"All it takes is one little dream and a huge chunk of belief."

T K McMillan

If you can throw your belief system behind your dreams you will make them a reality, never giving up the fight, never losing time on your efforts.....taking you to a place of self discovery.

My Day /

"Not everyone will believe you in the beginning.......but they will in the end."

T K McMillan

People don't believe in what they can't see, but once you show them, they'll be there with you.

My Day /

"Most people don't have vision for their own dreams, so be patient when they can't see yours."

T K McMillan

If we believe then really, that's all that matters. People may struggle to understand the picture you're trying to paint, so take time and be clinical in your explanation........especially if you need them to buy in.

My Day /

"When building a jigsaw you first must lay the outlines, then you move to the more in depth detail.........so too we must lay out our Goals."

T K McMillan

Lay out the foundations, get your initial structure in place..........then get to building your dream.

My Day /

"If we can capture it in our minds, we will hold it in our hands."

T K McMillan

If you can visualize your dream, and hold the image clearly in your mind each and every day, YOU will make it a reality!

My Day /

"In the end the only person's view that really matters........is YOURS."

T K McMillan

Regardless of wether people support your dream or doubt it, the only one who's vision must hold firm is your own. Do not be dissuaded if you believe you can make it happen.

My Day /

"This is a one off journey, you are not getting a re-run or a second go ....make it count first time round."

T K McMillan

Some days are better than others, in fact, some days are a million times better than others! But roll them all together and every step is worth it.........if we make it count.

My Day /

"If you don't like the colour of the walls, open another tin and get painting once again."

T K McMillan

If something isn't working do not linger or hesitate, review what it is that isn't working, consider what might be a better route, and then introduce change as quickly as you can.

My Day /

"Change is the way of the World, it is not something to fear or shy away from."

T K McMillan

The natural instinct is to stick with what we know.......just as the dinosaurs did! We must not only be prepared for change, but we must encourage it, that is where our growth lies.

My Day /

"What unique talent do you possess, what sets you apart from the rest?"

T K McMillan

Do you ever consider what individual talent you have that you don't see in others, something you know that you have that little bit extra of............and crucially, do you put it to good use?

My Day /

"Can you afford yourself some time today to work specifically on your dream?"

T K McMillan

Even if it's only 30 mins, at the beginning, middle or end of your day........take time out to apply yourself to learning a new skill or developing a current one.

My Day /

"There is no such thing as limited potential. If you are good enough, and you have the belief system, anything is possible."

T K McMillan

Do not run the risk of setting up unnecessary boundaries, do not restrict your Goals or thinking because of other people's standards.

My Day /

"Break through the ice."

T K McMillan

It may take an almighty push but once you go beyond that tipping point you know then that success can be yours. Keep going until it is done.

My Day /

"Am I convincing enough, can others see what I see?"

T K McMillan

If you are looking for support you must learn to portray your dream in a tangible fashion, in a manner that others can grasp on to.

My Day /

"Even Mount Everest was overcome."

T K McMillan

Regardless of the test, if you are determined enough and hungry enough, you will reach the peak.

My Day /

"Don't be afraid of being No.1.......somebody has to do it."

T K McMillan

For many of us we'd prefer to stop short of first place, hiding in the shadows content as runner up...........do not be afraid, you too can be the people's choice.

My Day /

"Never underestimate the depth of your own capabilities."

T K McMillan

We are too quick to assess that we ourselves are not worthy of winning the greatest prize however, until tested, we don't always get to see just what we are actually capable of.

My Day /

"People use all means of interaction to advertise someone else's product, but how do we use our time to advertise ourselves?"

T K McMillan

Remember this is a journey that begins and ends at your front door, so before you promote your next designer label, make sure you do it with no less enthusiasm than you have for your very own.

My Day /

"Do something meaningful with your time here........."

T K McMillan

This is your movie, you are the star attraction, you are the one they've all come to see.........
So make it a viewing worth watching.

My Day /

"You won't climb to the top without taking the first step."

T K McMillan

Getting started is often the most difficult part, but once you've made that opening move then you are off and running.

My Day /

"You begin training for a sprint race until you realize you can win a marathon."

T K McMillan

Once we achieve a little success............followed by another, we start to realize we are capable of way much more than we allowed ourselves to imagine.

My Day /

"We all hope to be a winner.......but how many of us really believe we can be?"

T K McMillan

We often carry the luggage of failure through our growing years, without understanding this as experience instead of defeat.

My Day /

"You are currently under training preparing for a bigger test........so don't get bogged down with momentary set backs."

T K McMillan

We can all become consumed in the moment.......good and bad, but that is not yet the end of our journey, so regardless, move ahead with the head held high.

My Day /

"I am healthy in living therefore I am wealthy in life."

T K McMillan

If you are spending your days doing what makes you happy, surrounded by the people who matter the most, you have immeasurable wealth..........not everything is counted in dollars and cents.

My Day /

"Our life's purpose lies in our own hands, do what fulfills you, not what fulfills someone else."

T K McMillan

Frequently people live doing what makes others happy, and of course in life there has to be an element of that, but don't live someone else's dream............live yours!

My Day /

"Every day is a school day."

T K McMillan

Every day provides us with the opportunity to learn, to grasp something for the first time and to develop our skill set further.........do not take it for granted, it's you who benefits most.

My Day /

"The more we learn, the more we seek."

T K McMillan

The more knowledge we obtain the more we realize we do not know, which leads us to cry out for more information, more opportunities to expand our mind.

My Day /

"You are born.........the rest is down to cashing in on good opportunities, don't wait for gifts."

T K McMillan

We shouldn't look for a sliver spoon moment, gifted the chance of privilege........if we want self made success then we must go and earn it."

My Day /

"Dedication and passion will open more doors than talent and laziness ever will."

T K McMillan

How many people do we encounter who are wasteful with their gifts, gifts most of us would cherish..........don't be one of those people, use what you have and give it your all.

My Day /

"It all boils down to what you' prepared to do to make a difference."

T K McMillan

You cannot idly sit and wait for success, you must commit yourself to making something special take place, YOU must be the one to make the difference to your days.

My Day /

"As challenging as some days are, they will not deter me in my pursuit of my dreams."

T K McMillan

Some days can really throw us offline, tests that can force us back down the path when we least expect it.........but so long as our resilience is bold enough, and our Goals are clear enough, we will not rest until that winning line has been crossed.

My Day /

"I dare to cross the road so that I may discover what lies on the other side."

T K McMillan

Of course life can be safer if we stay indoors, if we live without risk and choose not to take any chances.......but think of what we may find anew if we will just take a little chance.

My Day /

"Dream that extra little bit........"

T K McMillan

Don't ever underestimate what you really can achieve.........it's all out there and there is no reason YOU can't make it big.

My Day /

"There's a great difference between desire and will.........desire is wanting something, will is never giving up until you get it."

T K McMillan

We hold our dreams and aspirations close but how many of us truly do all we can to achieve them........give that genuine thought and see if you need to up your game.

My Day /

"You may be a lot closer than you think you know........now is not the time to give up."

T K McMillan

In moments of frustration we feel like we have nothing left to offer but, in fact, most major successes have come at that point just beyond where all seemed lost........give it that extra 10%, it may be just what you need.

My Day /

"You may be a lot closer than you think you know........now is not the time to give up."

T K McMillan

In moments of frustration we feel like we have nothing left to offer but, in fact, most major successes have come at that point just beyond where all seemed lost........give it that extra 10%, it may be just what you need.

My Day /

"Apply your time to the areas that develop you the most........we all have the same time, it's just that some people use it better than others.

T K McMillan

It's easy to lounge around when we could be researching or learning more in a beneficial way, we all love to relax......but we will only develop where we apply ourselves, so we must use our time wisely.

My Day /

"Your attitude and approach to almost any problem will determine its outcome before you even begin!"

T K McMillan

When you approach a challenge with a defeatist attitude you will have lost already, the moment you view it as a minor bump you will stride over it as though it was never there.

My Day /

"Do what you need to do to get there, do not afford yourself lame excuses, give it your very best shot."

T K McMillan

We can always find reason to not give something our level best, find others to blame and ways of letting ourselves off the hook........but if so we are only cheating ourselves, no one else loses more.

My Day /

"The journey is everything."

T K McMillan

What we will learn about ourselves as we walk through life is of far greater importance than the destination in itself, who it will form us into and what we will offer as a result.

My Day /

"Cherish the moments and remember the steps."

T K McMillan

We don't always recognize great moments in our lives as they occur, it's not until later we look back and see what a great occasion that time has been.........try to seize the special times in life.

My Day /

"Falling down is not a travesty, not getting back up is."

T K McMillan

We all fail some of the time but it's your enthusiasm for getting back up that shall reveal to you who you really are.

My Day /

"As sure as darkness will fall, the sun shall rise again."

T K McMillan

Sometimes we just need a new perspective on things, time to rest our heads and the opportunity to view our challenges anew. Don't give up, tomorrow's another day.

My Day /

"Sometimes to allow space for a new habit, you must first give up an old one."

T K McMillan

Once you know something isn't going to work in that way, re-assess, work a new strategy and move on with speed.

My Day /

"For an idea to grow it must be able to be understood by the audience you aim it at."

T K McMillan

Many ideas fail because they are too complicated for many people to follow, if you want a great number to understand you, keep it simple.

My Day /

"Stop looking over your shoulder, yesterday has gone, it's what you do today that's going to make a difference."

T K McMillan

We spend too much of our thinking time in the past.......learn from your errors and move forward with new zest.

My Day /

"Retaining a strong mindset in the face of adversity is a strength of few, but it is also a skill that can be developed with positive, conscious thinking."

T K McMillan

Being able to take a moment out and clearly assess a situation in its own merit will prevent panic or irrational thinking........control your thoughts, don't let them control you.

My Day /

"A person's value is not to be measured by the moment in which they stand, but by the years of effort and learning it has taken to get them there."

T K McMillan

We often look at the price of a service or value of a person in the specific moment we look at them, but, the true cost, is how they got there.

My Day /

"Behind the debris awaits your path."

T K McMillan

Sometimes we have to fight our way through the rubble to discover the treasure that lies beyond it.

My Day /

"Now is as good a time as any to get started on your dreams........."

T K McMillan

Make lists, make plans.......review them, adjust them, work on them.......do this with frequency and consistently and get moving towards your Goals.

My Day /

"Who you can become matters a great deal more than who you have been."

T K McMillan

As long as you have been gifted with another day above ground you still have the opportunity to improve on where you are at now.

My Day /

"Pay attention to people's behavior, is says a lot more about them than the words they speak."

T K McMillan

What people do on a consistent basis will reveal to you who they really are, friend or foe!

My Day /

"Don't measure your achievements against another's efforts, measure them against your own."

T K McMillan

Don't become embroiled in chasing what you see others have, it's what YOU want that matters most.

My Day /

"Speaking is a great way to help another but listening is the best way to help yourself."

T K McMillan

We all love the opportunity to present our views, but if we listen to that of another we may just learn something we don't already know.

My Day /

"Spend time with people who help to broaden your view."

T K McMillan

The most limiting thing we can do to ourselves is close our mind to a one tracked opinion......open your ears and you'll open your eyes.

My Day /

"Our ambitions can drive us to what we want, whilst our gratitude can give us thanks for what we have."

T K McMillan

Whilst we pursue our dreams we must always remember to take stock of what we have.......
Begin each day with sincere gratitude for who and what you are.

My Day /

"If you can bring out the best in someone, whilst they bring out the same in you........you know then you have a partner to grow with."

T K McMillan

Be it personal or in your career, ensure you surround yourself with people who drive you to do better, and if you can, try to repay the compliment back to them.

My Day /

"Thinking time and working time shouldn't always be at the same time."

T K McMillan

When you need to apply yourself with clear focus it is important you have no distractions.......an hour served alone in this way can be more beneficial than 2 hours in the workplace.

My Day /

"Example comes in what you do, not in what you say."

T K McMillan

Those who hold us in esteem will follow more our behavior than the words we actually say, be conscious of the example you are setting.

My Day /

"Whatever your competitors are doing, make sure you are doing more."

T K McMillan

You only need worry about the competition if they are outworking YOU, and if so, you need to up your game.

My Day /

"If your current results aren't what you desire, you must take time to invest in yourself, learn more, put time into your plans and the pay off shall prove its worth."

T K McMillan

We lose a lot of time wandering, hoping for improvement, wishing for things to get better......but unless we are actually investing time into ourselves, all will stay the same.

My Day /

"What we will receive shall be determined by what we can offer."

T K McMillan

Before we can expect to gain returns we must be satisfied in what we have to offer, in what we can contribute and in who we can help.

My Day /

"The only examination you need pass is the one you set yourself."

T K McMillan

Your conscience and your achievements must run parallel to your way of thinking..........don't be sucked in to competing with other people's achievements, only measure against your own.

My Day /

"If you want your house to stand up to the storms, make sure you build it well."

T K McMillan

We will face tough tests in life but the better we are prepared and the deeper our foundations of knowledge are, the more secure we will be when we need to fight back.

My Day /

"Just for a moment........imagine you have made it."

T K McMillan

Visualize yourself in the place you're trying to reach, see yourself as the success you wish to be......now how do you feel?!

My Day /

"You have time to grow, be sure to put it to good use."

T K McMillan

We each have the same twenty four hours in a day, how we use them shall determine where we end up.

My Day /

"Where lies my application?"

T K McMillan

Where is your focus, what efforts are you making to contribute to a better future, what new learning are you out there seeking?

My Day /

"Be at your best."

T K McMillan

When the opportunity comes, as it will surely do, be ready to step up and take your chance.

My Day/

"We can come through it."

T K McMillan

Regardless of how tough things can become there is always a path through the trouble. Be patient, you'll find the way.

My Day /

"The best days have not yet come."

T K McMillan

Stop looking back, stop reflecting on what you could have done.......live in the now, create new memories!

My Day /

"Call on all your experiences, good and bad."

T K McMillan

Learn from what you've gathered, use it to your advantage, and forge ahead with what's still to come.

My Day /

"Start the day as the sun comes up, not as it sets."

T K McMillan

Be ready to get going as brightly and as early as you can, don't lose half the day pondering.

My Day/

"Prepare for the battle......before you have to head into the trenches."

T K McMillan

The best preparation guarantees the greatest success.......be ready for the tough days, before they arrive at your door.

My Day /

"Water breaks through because it doesn't know how to stop trying."

T K McMillan

If you are prepared to apply continuous force, undying effort.......your breakthrough will come.

My Day /

"So what shall today's obstacles teach us?"

T K McMillan

If we can approach our day with this state of mind, we will surpass all that comes our way.

My Day /

"You won't lose who you don't need."

T K McMillan

People will come and go in your life but the one's who stay around are the one's worth hanging on to........for they are the one's who believe in you most.

My Day /

"What can become of me......?"

T K McMillan

Have you asked yourself that.......honestly?! Just how far do YOU think you can go?

My Day /

"Where is it you're headed?"

T K McMillan

Have you really given it a whole lot of thought..........where it is you are at least trying to end up?

My Day /

"What would you hope to gain from your travels?"

T K McMillan

As you move through the gears of life, what is it you hope to achieve.........who is it you aim to become?

My Day /

"Tunnel vision will keep you in the dark."

T K McMillan

You cannot afford to be narrow minded, it is imperative that you are able to consider someone else's viewpoint........otherwise how will you grow?

My Day /

"YOU will know when the time feels right."

T K McMillan

Regardless of how many times someone else attempts to tell you, or even encourage you......only YOU shall truly know when the time is exactly right.

My Day /

"You build a house from the bottom up, not the top down."

T K McMillan

It is imperative to get the structure right, no shortcuts, no cutting corners......do it right and it'll last the test of time.

My Day /

"There's always an easier way in the short term, but is it best for the long....."

T K McMillan

We can look for the easy way to success but, it's who we become whilst we grow that matters, more than the destination itself.

My Day /

"You may have to roll your sleeves up more than once you know...."

T K McMillan

Don't think because you've overcome one major obstacle the job is done, this is a long journey we are looking at, not a short sprint.

My Day /

"When temper is shown the fight is lost."

T K McMillan

Don't show your hand, control your emotions and control your behavior."

My Day /

"Who's in control of your next move?"

T K McMillan

Are you the sole driver of your own bus, are you planning your future.........or are the controls in the hands of another?

My Day /

"We can achieve a lot with our time here."

T K McMillan

If we apply ourselves with thought it is incredible the impact we can have, the good we can do, the journey we can embark upon.

My Day /

"Never measure yourself on what the competition scored."

T K McMillan

Personal development is based on how you do and what you're working on......what others are doing has no bearing on that.

My Day /

"Perseverance knows no boundaries."

T K McMillan

If you will keep going long enough the walls you face shall come tumbling down.

My Day /

"For a team to succeed so must the individual players within it."

T K McMillan

In any team, in any profession, each individual must care and fight equally against their own individual battles........and then collectively, victory shall come.

My Day /

"You alone are your greatest chance at success.."

T K McMillan

Don't expect your success to come at someone else's hand, you must be the one to drive your own success story forward.

My Day /

"It is in times of great adversity we realize what we value most."

T K McMillan

Sometimes, when we hit a bit of a stumble or we're thrown back a little, we become more aware of what we already really have.

My Day /

"We shall not be judged by how hard we fall, but in how we put the pieces back together."

T K McMillan

It goes wrong for us all at some point along the way, that's to be expected........but how you react is what shall define you, not the setback itself.

My Day /

"If you can soar above the clouds you'll discover the beautiful skies."

T K McMillan

When you're working hard, and fighting the daily battles that come to you, it doesn't always feel that the rewards are going to come.........but they will, if you just keep going.

My Day /

"If a bird can fly through changing seasons, so can YOU!"

T K McMillan

Times change and so do the tests that come with them, we must be well prepared for that and ready to adjust quickly.

My Day /

"If a bird can fly through changing seasons, so can YOU!"

T K McMillan

Times change and so do the tests that come with them, we must be well prepared for that and ready to adjust quickly.

My Day /

"Even when the foundations are laid the build can still be changed."

T K McMillan

Just because you've laid out your plan doesn't mean you can't change the route along the way.....things will happen that will require you to adjust your thinking, and your actions.

My Day /

"A purpose shall see you through when will is put to the test."

T K McMillan

If you have something, or someone, worth fighting for you will find the strength when you are going through the toughest of times.

My Day /

"Someone getting there first doesn't make it any less great."

T K McMillan

Just because you weren't first to achieve something or reach a Goal, doesn't demean the value of the achievement.........getting there is what really counts in the end.

My Day /

"It's time to wake up........"

T K McMillan

No more excuses, no weak reasoning........get out there and make things happen.

My Day /

"Make sure regret doesn't see you out the door."

T K McMillan

Don't be at the end feeling sorry for yourself because of what you could have been.......be active and make a difference whilst you can.

My Day /

"There is more I have yet to accomplish."

T K McMillan

Regardless of how far you feel you are down the road don't settle........ever! This is about life experiences remember, so pack them in!

My Day /

"Be decisive."

T K McMillan

Go for it, don't make feeble excuses so that you can continue to wander......get your plan down in front of you and go make something of yourself.

My Day /

"Wars are not won by the toughest of people, but by the smartest."

T K McMillan

Our ability to punch harder than the next guy will only be effective if we are sure to pick the right battles.

My Day /

"Be honest.......are YOU doing enough?"

T K McMillan

Is your contribution as great as it could be, are you giving all you can, and most of all, are you happy with the results you are getting?

My Day /

"Commit."

T K McMillan

No half measure, no luke warm contributions........once you've decided what you want to do, give it every ounce you can and don't let yourself down.

My Day /

"There's a lot we can do with our time here."

T K McMillan

Each represents a new opportunity, another chance, a fresh page.........value it as the gift it is and pursue it as though it's your last.

My Day /

"What matters most.........?"

T K McMillan

What and who drives you, what is your sense of purpose and who will you share the joy with?

My Day /

"You only have to view the life of a caterpillar to see how things can turn out."

T K McMillan

In moments of doubt it can be a challenge to cling on to the vision of success, that beautiful moment that lies over the hill that you so yearn...........but it's there, if you can only hang in long enough.

My Day /

"Applied focus makes anything a possibility."

T K McMillan

If you will apply your thinking to a specific target, and have a continuous measurement tool along the way, you will breach any goal you may set.

My Day /

"I am not here to simply repeat the same experiences on a day to day basis."

T K McMillan

We were not gifted with a place on this earth to just meander through each day........get out there and put yourself to the test, explore what may be seen, what may be touched.

My Day /

"Some things you have to learn along the way........."

T K McMillan

You can't figure it all out on a sheet of paper, some of it you have to learn on the job.

My Day /

"Take your chance."

T K McMillan

When the opportunity comes knocking, you be sure to be ready to grab it with both hands!

My Day /

"Do more than is asked of you."

T K McMillan

If you want to stand out, if you want be noticed, make sure you are outworking the competition and never the slacker at the back.

My Day /

"Keep climbing."

T K McMillan

When we experience some success it's easy to want to hesitate for a moments reward......but don't rest there for too long, there is much still to be achieved.

My Day /

"Be thankful."

T K McMillan

We can often get caught up in what we don't have but we should always start our day with a moments gratitude for all the great things we already do have.

My Day /

"Keep up the fight."

T K McMillan

Some days are longer than others, the work seems tougher and the end seems further away.......
But keep going, you are much closer than you think.

My Day /

"There is always another way......"

T K McMillan

If a particular route is not working out, stop, take time out, and reconsider the pathway you are pursuing.

My Day /

"It's never about where you start......"

T K McMillan

Where your journey begins doesn't have to be a reflection on where you end up........what you do in between will be what determines that.

My Day /

"It is easy to criticize from the safety of your own comfort zone."

T K McMillan

We can all see the fault in others, often quicker than we can in ourselves......but never criticize someone who is trying, especially whilst you are not.

My Day /

"Create something greater than thyself."

T K McMillan

What is it that people will remember you by, what are you doing now that can live on beyond your time here?"

My Day /

"There is no greater gift than peace of mind."

T K McMillan

It's been said to me in the past, "Do the right things for the right reasons and you won't go far wrong." Having a clear conscience comes from doing what's right whenever you can.

My Day /

"Determination is an incredible source of encouragement."

T K McMillan

Have you ever been so determined to do a thing you just know deep inside you will not fail, that you will not give up until the job is done? Harness that feeling so that you may call upon it when required.

My Day /

"Sometimes you have to tear up the script and write it over."

T K McMillan

It doesn't always work out at first attempt....even second or third, but if you will adjust your thinking, look at things from a different perspective......the solution will lie before you.

My Day /

"You can't discover gold without first getting your hands dirty."

T K McMillan

If you are not prepared to dig a little deeper, to fight a little longer, then the rewards you are chasing may remain out of reach.

My Day /

"Ride upon the clouds."

T K McMillan

Some days the storms come heavy, but these are the days of our greatest tests.......will you submerge below the clouds or shall you rise above them?

My Day /

"Cobbled roads are far more intriguing than flat motorways."

T K McMillan

All the bumps we endure along the way make for a far more rewarding destination.

My Day /

"Being single minded is not a selfish act, but a committed one."

T K McMillan

Focusing upon a goal doesn't mean that you will neglect other aspects of your life, or indeed the people in it, it simply means that your application on the target will be at its finest.

My Day /

"If you don't grasp the value of your skills you could end up in the hands of those that do."

T K McMillan

It is very difficult to measure the value of your own abilities, to exceed humility and know your own true worth........but don't allow that to leave you open for exploitation at the hands of someone who does.

My Day /

"An inner passion to succeed will leave every challenge in its wake."

T K McMillan

Even when faced with the toughest of obstacles, if you have a burning desire to succeed, you WILL make it.

My Day /

"Energy comes when positives attract."

T K McMillan

We are always searching out the like minded people among us, people we both relate to and connect with.......the one's whose positive vibes switch on our light.

My Day /

"What you KNOW matters much less than what you DO."

T K McMillan

Sitting around, with all your positive thoughts and great ideas, will make no possible difference without YOU taking action.

My Day /

"The dream only dies when YOU extinguish the flame."

T K McMillan

The moment you give up is the moment your dream dies a death. If it's not working out the way you want, review what you are doing........don't give up!

My Day /

"You can become no more than you envisage."

T K McMillan

If you cannot see yourself in the moment of victory how can you possibly expect to get there?"

My Day /

"History is reinvented with every passing day."

T K McMillan

Regardless of how good or bad your past achievements have been, they can be improved with each new day..........don't rest on old successes."

My Day /

"If you don't face the questions you'll never discover the answers."

T K McMillan

I know it can be tough to put yourself in the line of fire, but if you don't take a regular inventory of your behavior you will never grow.

My Day /

"Just because the outer layer is gentle doesn't mean there isn't a warrior lying within."

T K McMillan

You don't always have to expose all that is going on within, it's ok to be nice whilst winning!

My Day /

"Knowing someone will stand as your brother doesn't always require that you share the same blood."

T K McMillan

Some of the most reliable people in our lives are friends found along the way, people who share a similar passion for life and a genuine desire to help others.

My Day /

"The rain may be falling hard, but it can't last forever."

T K McMillan

In the toughest of times sometimes we can do no more than simply hang in there, surviving until the storm passes and a glimmer of sunshine reappears.

My Day /

"Just because the outer layer is gentle doesn't mean there isn't a warrior lying within."

T K McMillan

You don't always have to expose all that is going on within, it's ok to be nice whilst winning!

My Day /

"The winning post is not behind you."

T K McMillan

Stop looking back, the direction you're headed lies ahead!

My Day /

"Don't compare your results with those at the bottom of the leaderboard."

T K McMillan

It's easy to try to lift your poor results by comparing them to those not as equipped as yourself, but that won't help your growth, only the ones at the top will do that.

My Day /

"Deal with the root and you will deal with the problem."

T K McMillan

It's not enough to deal with problems on the surface, you must get in to the guts of them to eliminate the real issue.

My Day /

"Leave your mark."

T K McMillan

What can you do to ensure your contribution is remembered, what difference can YOU make to the project or person you engage with?

My Day /

"Even though our Goals lie in the future, we must remember to live in the now."

T K McMillan

We can sometimes get a little too ahead of ourselves but we must remember that today may be all we have, so live exactly there.

My Day /

"Daily dedication and application brings dreams to life."

T K McMillan

A continuous work ethic will breathe the necessary air into your dreams to make them your reality.

My Day /

"Cultivate faith, not fear."

T K McMillan

It's as easy to generate a positive, happy thought as it is one of fear or doubt.........control your mind and your actions will follow suit.

My Day /

"Stick to the point."

T K McMillan

Don't over complicate your plan, don't go beyond something that you cannot follow.......keep it simple and keep it precise.

My Day /

"Where is your current circle taking you.........?"

T K McMillan

Look around you, are the people you spend most time with inspiring you, or are they dragging you down?!

My Day /

"Even in my darkest days I face sleep only with thoughts of how I shall approach tomorrow."

T K McMillan

When times are low it is of even greater importance to work out a solution to your current situation.......don't bury your head, get your sleeves rolled up and get ready to go again.

My Day /

"Trust in where you are, the job is not yet done."

T K McMillan

Do not settle for mediocrity, do not rest on your laurels, this is a lifelong journey not just a short period of minimal successes.

My Day /

"My passion for victory is greater than my concern of a loss."

T K McMillan

Of course things will not work out perfectly every time, a stumble here, a stumble there........but the victory lies in the bigger picture, not just in the small incidentals.

My Day /

"The time is ticking by.........."

T K McMillan

The time is passing anyway, why not make it a constructive use of your time, a journey of exploration......not just a wandering repetition of your days.

My Day /

"If there is no sense of value, there is no sense at all."

T K McMillan

Our skills and attributes are gained and grown over a long period of time........don't treat them with less value than you deserve and be sure no one else does either.

My Day /

"Make time to reflect, but not linger."

T K McMillan

We must always make time to reflect on our efforts, sometimes even to question the depths of our results..........but know when to move on, do not hang about in places of self pity.

My Day /

"A new day is dawning."

T K McMillan

Each day is a fresh start, another chance........a day of opportunities, if you will only choose to see it as such.

My Day /

"Often the only thing stopping you...........is YOU!"

T K McMillan

Moments of self doubt are normal, we are all human you know. But, what have you got to lose, what is there really that allows you to be held back?

My Day /

"Tiredness can slow us down, but ambition will raise us once again."

T K McMillan

When you feel beaten, when the days seem drawn out ......afford yourself a rest, but remember the value of your dreams........get up, lift your spirit, and charge ahead once again.

My Day /

"When who you say you are doesn't match who you show you are people will quickly see right through you."

T K McMillan

If you're going to talk a good game, make sure you can walk it too.

My Day /

"Success is enjoyed on a much greater level when experienced alongside another."

T K McMillan

It doesn't only have to be about you, whether with a business partner or a personal one.......the joy is so much greater when achieved with a soul mate.

My Day /

"Can you see your efforts without the judgement of success or failure?"

T K McMillan

If you are able to view what you have done, or indeed what you are doing, without the burden of point scoring, would they benefit you more, would it be possible to learn more from them?

My Day /

"If it doesn't work for you, don't get involved."

T K McMillan

Almost from childhood people try to sway us to do things that go against our better judgement. We are on our journey, not their's....so trust your gut and stand your ground.

My Day /

"Nothing enthuses positivity like the company of a positive person."

T K McMillan

Spend as little time as possible with negative people, they will drag you down and drain you of the energy of which you so desperately require.

My Day /

"Measure your Goals against your own bar, not that of others."

T K McMillan

We can easily get caught up in other people's targets and standards, but what others do doesn't develop us........only what WE do does that.

My Day /

"If you can't lift your head you'll never lift your spirit."

T K McMillan

When we are in our lowest moments it can be difficult to get our head up and face the challenges, but if we don't our spirits shall stay in the ground so up we must rise!

My Day /

"The upside of the struggle is who you become."

T K McMillan

When you have to fight a little to gain your success it's not the trophy that makes it worth it, but the person it shapes you in to.

My Day /

"Criticism without a solution is neither worth saying or hearing."

T K McMillan

It is easy for of us to criticize the actions or behavior of another, but if we can offer no better solution we only serve to throw negativity upon an already negative situation.

My Day /

"What shall I gain for tomorrow as a result of what I did today?"

T K McMillan

What fruits are you planting for tomorrow, what actions do you undertake today to guarantee tomorrow is a step forward in your journey?

My Day /

"If you will take the time, you will take the rewards."

T K McMillan

We don't always want to put the time in, to practice, to research, to learn........but having the dedication and persistence is what will set us apart from the rest.

My Day /

"If your book is to be worthy of purchase, your story must be worthy of reading."

T K McMillan

If you want people to believe and invest in you then you must offer something in return. People must be able to see where is the worth of their time and commitment.

My Day /

"We know of many a success story that began with humbler beginnings than ourselves."

T K McMillan

For many of us the excuse not to try is that "it couldn't happen for us", but we know deep down that's not really the case.........it's never about where someone begins, but about where they finish.

My Day /

"Your time may pass but your influence shall not."

T K McMillan

When our time has gone what do we leave behind, how are we to be remembered.......because, be it positive or negative, a mark shall be left all the same.

My Day /

"Sometimes courage is born out of the need to fight back."

T K McMillan

When we are left with few other options but to fight back we display our greatest inner strengths, abilities we may not have discovered if it were not for our lack of alternatives,

My Day /

"It hasn't taken the discovery of DNA for you to understand how unique you are!"

T K McMillan

We each have unique talents and abilities we have been gifted with, what we do with them is what makes them special.

My Day /

"Occasionally it is necessary to STOP, and take stock of where the tide is taking you."

T K McMillan

It is too easy to just go with the flow, wandering into places you didn't truly intend going........take control of YOUR direction and be sure it's what you want.

My Day /

"If you want to see different results you may have to dramatically change your behavior."

T K McMillan

We must always be honest with ourselves, taking a regular inventory of what is working for us and what is not.........and where necessary, have the courage to change where necessary.

My Day /

"Not everyone is worthy of being taken at face value."

T K McMillan

We are born optimists so we naturally give people the benefit of the doubt, but tread with care, they don't ALL deserve it.

My Day /

"Sometimes you have to really look at things, not as you wish them to be, but in how they truly are."

T K McMillan

We look at many things in life in the way we'd like to see them, but in truth, that's not how they in fact are.

My Day /

"How far have you come?"

T K McMillan

When you review this latest period of personal development, what will you cherish most, what highs and lows have you to reflect on, and what will you do with what you now know?

My Day /

"Sometimes you have to bare your teeth."

When you are pushed back by someone for the wrong reasons, when you are being deliberately intimidated to weaken your strong position, you may just have to stand up ....and stand firm!

My Day /

"Don't carry last year's luggage into this year's journey."

T K McMillan

As you get ready to take upon a new journey be sure to let it start afresh, having learned from yesterday's mistakes, but without burdening yourself with their disappointment.

My Day /

With special thanks to my loving wife Anita and our three amazing children, without their continued support my dreams would also lay unfulfilled.

Also to my parents Tommy and Frances, the loving and secure environment they brought myself and my two sisters up in has allowed us each to grow in our own individual ways...........
I will always lay indebted that they had a friend in Bill W.

Please look out for my future books from The Daily Diary Series,

With sincerest gratitude for taking the time to read my offerings,

Thomas x

Printed in Great Britain
by Amazon